Jubilation on the Journey

by

Margaret M. Stevens

Spiritual Solutions for Today's Challenges

"Jubilation on the Journey"

Publisher:

THE MARGARET STEVENS INSTITUTE
P.O. Box 3366
Ashland, Oregon 97520

Manufactured in the
United States of America.

Printed by
IPCO Printing Company
Ashland, Oregon

ISBN 0-9655888-0-7

Dedication

I lovingly dedicate this collection of thoughts and ideas to my dear friend, Lucy Martin Wener, with deep appreciation for her friendship. Her loving, generous support and encouragement have cheered me, inspired me, and enabled me to find more jubilation on my own journey.

Acknowledgements

My deep appreciation to Stephen Boyd for his invitation to contribute to his fine publication, LITHIAGRAPH, and for his willingness to let me share these articles which have appeared in it for the past several years.

Thanks to Ellen and Michael Weiland for their expertise and dedication in putting these ideas into print. Without these dear friends, this book would not have happened.

And to my sons, Rodger, for the foreword, and David, for the cover design.

My love and prideful appreciation.

Foreword

Have you ever toured a well-tended garden in the company of one who knows the plants? Such a person will be able to show and tell you things you never noticed, about those familiar plants you thought you understood.

The garden, in this case, features plants which are no strangers to us—the common, everyday experiences we humans find in our day-to-day worlds. And the gardener is a lady who has spent the major part of her life tending to the cares and concerns of people just like you and me.

Her simplicity and easy style belie the years she has spent learning her trade, and the clarity with which she reveals the hidden character of our experiences prompts us to look more closely . . . if she found it, perhaps we can find it as well . . .

This little book, therefore, is a bouquet of visions, an arrangement of life's flowers set in a a vase of love and compassion with an artist's touch.

Originally presented singly in the soil of the Ashland, Oregon Lithiagraph, they are here collected and presented in the expectation that many more of us might behold their charm and fragrance.

It is with a curious mixture of pride and humility that I write this foreword. Being a writer myself, I am once again delighted to discover anew the charm and grace of another's expression. In this case, however, the nuances carry added fragrance, for the gardener whose hand has penned these essays much earlier applied that hand to rearing me, for she is also my mother.

Enjoy —

Rodger Stevens

Table of Content

Jubilation

on the

Journey

PUTTING SPRING IN YOUR LIFE

"Delegating responsibility is not only good business practice, it is good life management--remember life will go on."

Spring a time when all nature renews herself, and yet people, the highest form of God's creation [that we are aware of] often seem oblivious to the miracle of rebirth going on all around them. Spring is the time to take stock of ourselves, to clear out the dark corners of our minds, the fears and misgivings and worries that may have haunted us through the dark winter months. It is the time for mental and spiritual house - cleaning, a time for reveling in the goodness of life and appreciating all the evidences of God's love.

A grandmother promised her small grandson that if the next day were warm and pleasant, with no cool breezes to aggravate her rheumatism, she would take him to the park. As the little boy knelt down for his usual bedtime prayer, he added, "And please, God, make it hot for Grandma tomorrow."

Here are a few of the spring cleaning techniques that have worked for me.

First, take some action in improving your physical being, treat your body with love and respect for the wonderful instrument that it is. A group of behavioral scientists used certain benign drugs on a group of elderly, slightly senile residents in a rest home. The drugs induced "massive doses of sleep" in people who were old and depleted before their time. The results were astounding, a remarkable regeneration of tissues, disappearance of several chronic diseases, and as a final result, there was a general feeling of well being and love of life. Wouldn't you be surprised if this simple remedy, a few massive doses of sleep, restored your zest for life?

Secondly, begin to train yourself to think of all the good and joyful conditions and events in your life, and build a strong expectation of even more good in the future.

Every day, no matter how dull and routine, has at least one high spot. Learn to look for these surprise packages that add zest to living. Dr. Emmet Fox wrote a little booklet, The Seven Day Mental Diet, in which he said, "Resolve that for seven days you will watch your words, that you will not say a single untrue, mean, or depressing thing." I shared his idea with a group of church women, and a few days later one lady called to say, "If I keep that seven day diet, I'll have to tape my mouth shut, it is impossible to follow such instructions." I assured her that was not an easy assignment, but that the more we practiced it, the less frequently unkind, untrue, hurtful words would roll off our tongues.

Consider the two most important moments of your day--the moment just before you open your eyes in the morning, and the moment just before you drop off to sleep at night--these are the brackets of your conscious day. If these precious moments are filled with positive, uplifting thoughts, your day will be productive and happy, and your nights, restful and peaceful. Emerson wrote: "Finish each day and be done with it. You have done the best you could. Some blunders, and absurdities no doubt crept in; forget them as soon as you can. Tomorrow is a new day, begin it well and serenely with too high a spirit to be cumbered with your old nonsense."

Thirdly, learn the joy and satisfaction of giving in the form of money, time, energy, love--anything that takes you out of yourself, and transfer the gift of yourself, helpfully, to others.

A very successful young man went to his doctor to find answers for his general malaise and lack of interest in life. After a few probing questions, his doctor said, "I am not surprised at your condition. You give nothing to anyone but your family, and you give them too much." The young man confessed that his reluctance to give was based on his insecurity about money, and sadly added that he had nothing of himself to give in terms of time and love and attention. The old doctor continued, "It is no wonder that you get no fun out of life. You've stopped the creative process. You're run down because everything is coming in and nothing is going out. You are like the Dead Sea, all inlets and no outlets, and that means stagnation."

These are the words the surprised young man found on the prescription slip the doctor handed him: "Increase your giving to your church, or charitable institutions to at least 10%, and begin giving to needy individuals, for which you can get no tax write-off. Stop rushing around long enough to really give yourself to people--kind words to your staff, the policeman on the corner, your wife and children. Get involved in some activity that helps others."

The young man followed this advice by offering his services to his minister, and the result was a regular schedule of calling on those in hospitals and rest homes. His joy became contagious, affecting many people, and his material success continued to escalate as he learned to share and to love and to enjoy life.

My friends, won't you enter into the resurrecting spirit of the season--rejoice in your own rebirth, physically, mentally, and spiritually!

God Bless you!

[April 1994]

LADY OF FAITH

"Then at a certain stage I began to realize . . . breast cancer is a hard example of how a positive change can come from a seemingly very negative thing. But in my case, and in countless others, the result has been so wonderful compared to what might have been."

You might say that Margaret Stevens entered the ministry by accident. "Only I don't believe," she says with conviction, "that there is such a thing as an accident. I think what really happened was that I stumbled upon the thing that was God's will for me."

A retired minister of an independent New Thought Church and now in her radiant seventies, Stevens was once a home-maker and active in church and community, while raising three children. At the time, she had no interest in going into the ministry as such. "I just started feeling that I'd like to be doing more and contributing more," she explains. "I was vaguely dissatisfied with my limited role, and that dissatisfaction was the beginning of what turned out to be my life's work!"

Margaret Stevens is quick to assert her belief that each person has a need to contribute whatever he or she can to the world, no matter how small that contribution might seem. "No one of us is here just to take up space. We all have a purpose. Each of us is connected to the Source. . ." She laughs, "My grandson calls it the Force!"

Asked where she acquired her deep spiritual beliefs, she turns serious again. "I was crippled and unable to walk at all from the age of ten to the age of thirteen. I'd fallen off a porch onto a concrete driveway and, as a result, developed a bone disease." The disease was osteomyelitis. Easily treatable with modern drug therapy, it was considered incurable when Margaret was a girl. "The doctors said I would never walk again. That was when my father introduced me to this way of life, though he had no label for it at the time. He taught me to visualize myself walking, to even pretend that I could walk, and walk again I did. I had a severe limp, because one leg was two and a half inches shorter than the other--but I walked."

Then, at the age of twenty-four, after the birth of her first child, Margaret Stevens experienced what she considers a divine healing. "My diseased leg began to grow! In the space of two years, it grew the two-and-a-half inches that it had lost. X-rays appeared [to indicate] nothing had ever been wrong. My doctors were astounded. It was a true medical miracle."

Margaret Stevens found in New Thought the teachings in which her father had believed but for which he never had a name. "It's about the metaphysical. The word means 'beyond the physical'. Unlike the philosophy of Christian Science, we don't deny the reality of illness or forego medical treatment. Rather, we recognize that there is a purpose behind it, and look for what lessons we can learn from it and what good can come about because of it."

Asked how New Thought explains illness and injuries in babies and young children, she explains, "There really are no pat answers for some things. Being a firm believer in reincarnation, I tend to think that we can be born still carrying with us a pattern from a former life. I don't believe such things are given to us as punishment, but as learning opportunities."

Margaret Stevens has long been convinced that there are no coincidences in life, that everything happens for a reason. "There simply are no accidents," she explains, "only connections that we do not see, and may never see in this lifetime. This point of view has always helped me to accept whatever comes my way, and not get angry or try to fight it. It simply makes life more peaceful."

Margaret Stevens describes the various world religions and philosophies, and even modern-day twelve-step programs, as all parts of the same process. "It's never a matter of this way being the only right way. There is good to be found in all paths, and a common thread runs through them all. I happen to have found the path that feels right for me at this time, after having originally been in traditional religion, I didn't quite find what I needed along that particular road, but I know of many people who certainly have. I'm all for anything that helps people develop their spirituality."

Three years ago, while serving her ministry in Arcadia, California east of Pasadena, Margaret Stevens was stricken with breast cancer that resulted in a mastectomy.

While confronting cancer, did her belief in the metaphysical waver? "No, I never stopped believing. Of course it came as a blow, and I found myself questioning the way we all tend to question such things. But I kept doing the best that I knew how to do, praying and affirming God's will for my greatest good. Then at a certain stage I began to realize something. Breast cancer is a hard example of how a positive change can come from a seemingly very negative thing. But, in my case and in countless others, the result has been so wonderful compared to what might have been."

Indeed, illness opened the doors for this thoughtful, easy speaking woman. Having been to Ashland just once, with her husbands approval and support she moved to Ashland, Southern Oregon, in 1993. Stevens visits her husband frequently, but seems to have firmly chosen to live in Ashland. "I wanted a new beginning, I've never been alone in my whole life--I'll be seventy-four in August--and I love this new life. I love Ashland, its openness, its people, its beauty. Cancer was the open door; it reaffirmed my belief in myself as more than just a body walking around. My body is only a vehicle-a spaceship, so to speak. It's what I get around in. It's the person on the inside, who is me!"

--Stevie Redfield [May 1994]

ART (AND CRAFT) OF IMAGING

"Prayer is a good way to combat anxiety and promote healing. When you pray, however you pray, you assume that there is some force in the universe which is on your side."

"Most men live lives of quiet desperation," so said a wise and insightful man many years ago. Perhaps you can identify with that statement, wanting conditions and things in your life that seem impossible to attain.

Have you tried using your incredible gift of imagination?

People often say, "But I have no imagination," and, if you are one of those people, remember the night your daughter was late coming home from a party, or the doctor gave you a slightly questionable diagnosis. What did your imagination do on those occasions? Didn't it run wild, conjuring up all sorts of dreadful possibilities which were hard to dispel?

Dr. Norman Vincent Peale, whose life was a testament to the wise use of this God-given faculty, said this: "Imagining is a kind of laser beam of the imagination, a shaft of mental energy in which the desired goal or outcome is pictured so vividly by the conscious mind that the unconscious mind accepts it and is activated by it. This releases powerful internal forces that can bring about everlasting changes in the life of the person who is doing the imaging."

Someone once said to me, "Isn't imaging simply trying to tell God what to do . . . taking too much responsibility on oneself? How can you know that you are imaging the right thing?"

My answer was this: "Where do you think you got the ability to image? You are part of the indescribable intelligence of God, or the Force, or whatever you choose to call a supreme being. You have been given the power to choose how you will use the gift, this marvelous creative ability. You are using it all the time, so why not be more conscious of how you are using it? Could your misuse of it be responsible for many problems that seem to plague you?"

One of my favorite stories illustrating this powerful tool is the one about a young soldier who was horribly wounded in WW II. He was brought into the field hospital, more dead than alive, and he remained that way even when transferred to a more equipped treatment center. All the medical care he received seemed ineffective and one day, in his attempt to make the endless, painful hours pass more quickly, he began to relive, in his mind, the happy times of childhood and youth.

He remembered his victories on the football field, the joy on his parents' faces when he received some special honor at school. He visualized these experiences vividly and, to his surprise, he forgot, momentarily, his pain and defeat. He also realized that each time he had scored a victory or gained an objective HE HAD A MENTAL PICTURE OF SUCCESS BEFORE IT HAPPENED. That very day Lew Miller began to visualize his complete recovery, "seeing" himself walking, happily married with a lovely family, working at a job he loved. He reasoned with himself this way, "We are essentially minds with bodies, not the other way around. Therefore my mind can dominate my body, so from this moment I will visualize recovery, my thoughts will steadily form and produce the physical counterpart of those thoughts."

It happened as he visualized. His recovery was slow, but it was complete, and all his mental pictures took form, fueled by enthusiasm, and sustained by faith and gratitude.

Dr. Irving Oyle has written: "Positive, beautiful thoughts trigger the release of beneficial hormones in the body, and these hormones help the body to heal itself. On the other hand, if you presume that you live in a hostile universe the reaction to that presumption wears out the body. Prayer is a good way to combat anxiety and promote healing. When you pray, however you pray, you assume that there is some force in the universe which is on your side. The minute you do that, your body relaxes, and the healing process begins. Faith itself creates the hormones that make you live longer."

A 90 year old man was killed in a traffic accident and, after the autopsy, the coroner said to the man's son, "Your father had all kinds of ailments and diseases that should have killed him long ago. Yet you say he was active and energetic until the day of the accident. How do you explain his long full life?" The son replied, "I can't explain it unless it was the result of his habit of saying, every morning of his life," Today is going to be a terrific day!"

Here are some simple suggestions for activating your imaging power:

• DISCARD THE FAILURE IMAGE. Failure is not a matter of permanent defeat. Failure is not trying again. Whenever you find the old, depressing pictures coming into your mind, instantly replace them with pictures of what you want.

• SET SOME NEW DEFINITE GOALS. Write them down-- what you want to accomplish, how you intend to get started, when you want the objective competed. Example: "By October 1st I will weigh 125 pounds, this goal to be accomplished by walking three miles a day, cutting down on sweets, and affirming my new health daily."

• BEGIN TO IMAGE, OFTEN AND INTENSELY, THE CONDITION YOU WANT TO SEE MANIFEST IN YOUR LIFE. See yourself, feel yourself, doing the things you want to do. Employ all the senses--feel the sea breeze on your face, the smell of ocean air, the sound of crashing waves, the restful scene of a vast sandy beach--all components of the vacation you want to enjoy.

BELIEVE THAT YOU HAVE ALREADY RECEIVED. "Act as if," said Shakespeare. "Assume a virtue if you have it not." Know that the universe is on your side. It is! Have fun with your imagination!

[July 1994]

STRESS-STOPPING STRATEGY

"Delegating responsibility is not only good business practice, it is good life management--remember life will go on."

With all that is going on in our world these days, one persistent subject seems to be in nearly everyone's conversation, and if they are not talking about it, they're thinking about it. Nearly every issue of every publication has something to say about it. The subject is pressure, the kind of pressure imposed upon us by outer conditions over which we seem to have no control, the kind which builds up within us, fueled by frustration and futility. Experts tell us that pressure and stress are here to stay, so we'd be wise to learn how to handle them successfully.

Pressure and stress can produce amusing or sobering responses in people. Expectant fathers are text-book examples. Consider the man who called his wife's obstetrician in the middle of the night to say that her labor had begun. The doctor asked, "Is this her first child." This distraught man replied, "No! This is her husband."

There seem to be two kinds of pressure. One is the kind we share with everyone else in society, just because we are human beings living in trying times. Everyday happenings seem to trigger pressure--the rising cost of living, whirlwind lifestyles, business competition, and on and on.

One authority on the subject has said, "The explosion of instantaneous communication is imposing a terrible stress upon us all. We are exposed to too many horror stories, information about fires, murders, and other distressing conditions. Primitive people usually faced one enemy at a time, but modern people are at the center of a threatening world which shows no sign of letting up on its threat to human happiness."

Now, add to these general pressure producers, your own personal concerns and worries, and you have a tremendous load to carry. We know that excess pressure, not handled properly, produces all kinds of physical problems, as well as inefficiency at work, psychosomatic symptoms, damaged relationships, social withdrawal, serious mental problems.

Let's look at the life of a familiar Bible character who wrestled with the problem of pressure thousands of years ago. [It was not a new human condition, even then.] Moses knew pressure which nearly finished him off several times. Even his father-in-law worried about him, and proposed a plan to help.

Moses' victory over pressure began when he listened to his father-in-law, a man older and wiser than himself, and one who was genuinely concerned about him. Of course, it took humility on Moses' part to accept help from a most unlikely source, especially since humility is not often part of the make up of a success-oriented person. Moses took the advice and began to delegate responsibility. His personal pressure was relieved, and the administration of the affairs of his people became more smooth and efficient.

Delegating responsibility wisely is not only good business practice, it is good life management. Of course, we often have to deal with an inflated ego that believes no one else can do the job as well as we can. It helps to remember that, if for some reason we couldn't do the job, life would go on. [A stress-relieving idea in itself.]

I would like to offer five simple steps which have helped me deal with pressure over the years. I hope they will prove helpful to you.

• ACCENTUATE THE POSITIVE: Spend some time each day mentally reviewing the things that are right in your world. Feel and express gratitude for the innumerable blessings you enjoy.

• ELIMINATE THE NEGATIVE: Watch your language for negative responses. Spend less time with hostile, negative people, unless you are strong enough to make a dent in their negativity.

• DO SOMETHING YOU REALLY ENJOY DOING: Budget

some time each week just for fun things--a favorite hobby, or sport; something that gives you a change of pace. Carl Rogers, the noted psychiatrist, once said, "A change is as good as a rest."

• ACCEPT YOURSELF: Be patient with yourself. It's okay to have a wart or two. Accept your flaws and limitations as part of your humanity, at the same time knowing that your true Self is divine and perfect.

• KEEP YOUSELF SPIRITUALLY WELL FED. Read good books, inspirational books, listen to uplifting music, enjoy the out-of-doors, and try to include these in your schedule each day. You can't eat enough food on Sunday to last you all week. You need daily refreshment, so take into your consciousness ideas, concepts, elevating thoughts, that will lift your awareness of your ability to meet and overcome any challenges you may have in your life.

God bless you!

[August 1994]

JUBILATION ON THE JOURNEY

"With all thy getting, get understanding." That understanding, I believe, is an appreciation of the joys and wonders of the journey, a recognition that the journey is a process. . ."

Have you ever said [or thought] things like this? "When I retire, I'll be happy. . . When the children are grown and on their own, life will be peaceful. . . I don't mind the long hours of work now--the end result will be worth it all." A friend, waiting to die, remarked, "If only I had taken more time to really live. I was so intent on reaching a certain social position, making lots of money, that I ruined my health, neglected important relationships, and missed out on so much that life had to offer . . . if only I could do it over again, I'd do it right!"

One of the wisest men who ever lived said this: "With all thy getting, get understanding." That understanding, I believe, is an appreciation of the joys and wonders of the journey, a recognition that the journey is a process, just as important as the final destination.

In the book of Exodus, we read of the 40 year wanderings of the Israelite people as they searched for the promised land that God had offered. A look at a map of that part of the world will conclude that there is much more to the story than just an ancient narrative about a persecuted people trying to escape. The wilderness in which they wandered was relatively small--roughly the size of the Rogue Valley. They bickered, complained and made Moses' leadership a nightmare. One wonders if their 40 year meanderings might have been greatly shortened if they had made the best of their situation, stopped running in circles, and paid more attention to Moses' guidance. Their story is our story. Don't we go over and over the same problems, covering the same territory, ignoring what good there might be in the experience? I have always felt sorry for poor Moses, to have put up with rebellion all those years, and then to die just before entering the promised land. Uppermost in the minds of the Israelites was the dangling carrot of their final destination, but they eventually realized that there is no final arrival. They lived on that promised land for some years, but then they were carried off into another dark period of slavery by the Babylonians.

Tucked away in our subconscious minds is an idyllic vision in which we see ourselves on a long journey spanning an entire continent. We're traveling by train, and from the windows we drink in passing scenes of cars on nearby highways, of children waving at crossings, of cattle in distant pastures, of city skylines and breath-taking sunsets. But uppermost in our conscious minds is our final destination, for at a certain hour on a given day, our train will pull into the station with flags waving and bands playing. Once that day comes all the pieces of our jigsaw lives will fit together, our dreams will come true. Restlessly we pace the aisles and count the miles, peering ahead, cursing the minutes for loitering, waiting, waiting, yes, when we reach that destination, that will be it. From that day on, we'll live happily ever after.

Sooner or later, however, we must realize that there is no station, no one place to arrive once and for all. The station is an illusion, constantly outdistancing us. But what about this moment, this day? When will we realize that the joy of the journey is the only joy of which we can be certain? The destination we envision may never materialize as we picture it. It didn't for Moses. . .

Suggestions for accepting the gifts of the present:

• REWORK THE SLOGANS BY WHICH YOU LIVE. Today the motto for many is "Go for the gold," used by Olympic competitors and others with that mind-set. We all need goals and incentives but perhaps a more satisfying motto might be "Relish the moment." This kind of motto moves us along toward our goal but also keeps us from wasting time pacing the floor and counting the miles.

• CHANGE GEARS AT APPROPRIATE TIMES. When you leave work, you change into the role of parent or partner. When you talk with your parents you become the son or daughter. The roles seem to shift too fast, troubles mount and magnify. Sometimes we have to shift into low gear, let the engine idle, seeking greater power when the situation demands, learning to coast at other times. Shifting gears is an art and enables us to get from, and give to, the most of every moment.

• LOOK FOR THE BLESSINGS IN EVERY EVENT AND SITUATION. The poet has said, "Of all sad words of tongue and pen, the saddest are these, "It might have been!" When you look for and find the sometimes obscure blessing in everything, you do not waste time thinking "what if ... if only. . ."

Yesterday is history, tomorrow is a mystery, Today is a gift, that's why they call it THE PRESENT. . .

[September 1994]

TRY THE LIGHT TOUCH

My favorite insight is one I have tried to live by for the past 40 years: 'Joy is the most infallible sign of the presence of God.' Not love, or peace, or power, but joy. Anyone can be lighthearted when everything is going smoothly.

Teilhard de Chardin was a Jesuit priest whose insights and revelations were far ahead of most of his contemporaries. My favorite insight is one I have tried to live by for the past 40 years: JOY IS THE MOST INFALLIBLE SIGN OF THE PRESENCE OF GOD. Note, he did not mention love, or peace. or power, but joy. Anyone can be lighthearted when everything is going smoothly. The test is this: How do you respond when life gets heavy? What is your reaction to trouble, unexpected detours in your path, disappointments?

It has long been my contention that we do an injustice to true religion, which emphasizes our oneness with the Creator, in whose image and likeness we are made, when we look at the dark side of everything.

I agree with de Chardin, and make every effort to lighten up, to remember his criterion for determining how clearly we identify with our divinity.

We're all familiar with the Peter Principle. Peter's educational law says this: "Experience is the worst teacher. It gives the test before explaining the lesson." Voltaire boldly offered his view that "the art of medicine consists of amusing the patient while nature cures the diseases." On an even lighter note, humorist Herb Shriner quipped "Our doctor would never operate unless it was absolutely necessary. He was just that way. If he didn't need the money, he wouldn't lay a hand on you!" [Apologies to our doctor friends.]

Nurse Deborah Lieber of Palo Alto has organized a new NFL [not another football league but Nurses for Laughter]. Their slogan is "Caution! Humor may be hazardous to your illness." Another nurse, Allison Crane of Chicago, has become a full-time humor consultant, and she writes: "The effects of laughter are similar to aerobic exercise--that is why we call it internal jogging."

"Facial muscles that activate smiles and laughter are connected with the thymus gland," states Dr. Annette Goodheart. "Without laugher, the thymus shrinks. Do you want a shrunken thymus, or a juicy, healthy one?" Dr. Goodheart blames rigid religions, with their mea culpa concept of sin, shame and guilt, for inhibiting the spontaneous joy and laughter in children and for suppressing the mirthful spontaneity that nature invokes in adults.

Dr. Joel Goodman, a 45 year-old free spirit, has organized the Humor Project in Saratoga Springs, New York, and has involved more than 20,000 participants in workshops and programs. He maintains that stress is not an event in itself, but a perception of an event, that people who use humor to cope with everyday problems don't show the kind of physiological responses to stress as the humorless. "It is the dead serious types that drop dead."

Without getting political, I think we all remember Ronald Reagan's clever use of humor at some tight spots in his Presidency. . . "Senator Jesse Helms wants me to move to the right. Sen. Lowell Weicker wants me to move to the left, and Sen. Ted Kennedy wants me to move back to California." When critics told Reagan he was too old to be President, he was ready with a quick reply: "Thomas Jefferson said one should not wonder about his exact chronological age relative to his ability to perform, and ever since he told me that..."

How do we begin to incorporate a new joy and lightness into our everyday lives? I suggest that we start the day with a feeling of expectancy of good. My favorite waking thought is this: "I just know that something wonderful is going to happen to me today!" And it always does.

Read good humor books, look for the humor in the things that happen to you. Try to develop a lighter perspective on life-don't give too much thought or energy to all the negative stories and reports in the media. You can do something positive and constructive about the dismal conditions by feeling the joy within your own being, and by sending out energies of joy and well-being to all of those around you, and beyond.

A friend recently sent me a small gray rock and told me to carry it with me always. On closer scrutiny, I saw the words CHOOSE JOY carved on one side. I do carry it with me and, when my fingers close around that little rock, I am happily reminded that I do have a choice as to how I will respond to events and conditions. Another friend wrote in a letter, "I know God never gives me more than I can handle, but sometimes I wish he wouldn't trust me so much."

Try starting your day with this simple advice from Opening the Door Within by Eileen Caddy: "What is your first thought on waking? Is it one of joy for another wonderful day or do you dread what the day might bring? Can you wake up with a song of praise and thanksgiving in your heart? What a difference it will make for you when you can do this, when you start the day by putting on rose colored glasses and seeing your day through them. Know that everything you say will be said with love, that everything you think will be the highest, and that nothing but the very best will be yours today. Let His joy be in you and let it be full!

[October 1994]

TRY THANKFULNESS

"We think loved ones are going to live forever and we put off saying the really important things to them. . ."

Snoopy is getting dog food for his Thanksgiving dinner and is aware that the family inside the house is enjoying turkey and all the trimmings. He meditates and talks to himself, "How about that? Everybody is eating turkey today, and because I'm a dog, I get dog food!" He trots away, positions himself on top of his doghouse and concludes, "It could have been worse. I could have been born a turkey."

There is no human emotion, with the possible exception of love, that brings as many benefits, tangible and intangible, as the spirit of thanksgiving. Just as love is the lubricant in hurtful situations, so thanksgiving is the dooropener to new opportunity and fulfillment. Some of the rewards of a thankful heart are these:

• HAVING A THANKFUL HEART WILL MAKE YOU A NICE PERSON. On the tombstone of her husband's grave, a simple mountain woman had chiseled in uneven letters: HE ALWAYS APPRECIATES. Can't you picture the kind of marriage those two enjoyed? Thankful people are always counting their blessings and they just naturally smile more.

• A THANKFUL HEART WILL ALERT YOU TO OPPORTUNITIES THAT SURROUND YOU AT ALL TIMES. One Thanksgiving I mentioned to my congregation the practice of giving thanks for everything in their lives--even the challenges and disappointments. One young woman called me two years later to tell her story. Bored with her routine job, she had gone through the motions for years, her mind occupied with thoughts of frustration. After my suggestion, she had begun to look for ways to improve her job, to do all her mundane operations in a spirit of thankfulness and gratitude. She was noticed by her supervisor, and in time became a member of the management staff, then a board member. As she happily told me her story, she concluded with, "Quite a change, don't you agree? And all because I began the simple practice of giving thanks for all things, even my boredom!"

• A THANKFUL HEART WILL HELP YOU OVER THE ROUGH PLACES IN YOUR LIFE. I have always loved this story told about the great composer, Beethoven. Did you know that the magnificent "Ode to Joy" was composed by a man whose affliction of deafness was an almost overwhelming handicap? When the deafness first came upon him, he wrote: "What a sorrowful life I must now live! I must draw back from everything and the most beautiful years of my life will take wings without accomplishing the promise of my talent and powers." Even while writing these words, there was, within this great soul a spirit that refused to whine for long. Now hear what he wrote later, after he had taken control of his worst fears. "There is no greater joy for me than to pursue and produce my art. I will seize fate by the throat. Most assuredly, it shall not get me entirely down. O, it is so beautiful to live life a thousand-fold."

• A THANKFUL HEART WILL ALERT YOUR MIND AND HEART TO PRESENT BLESSINGS. You can begin to experience the rewards of a thankful heart this very day:
Count your blessing--make a list and read it often.
Every night review your day, spending some time feeling grateful for the high moments and lessons learned.
Practice saying "thank-you" to people you have been taking for granted.

Practice looking for the good in every person and situation.

Watch your thoughts and words, eliminating the negative, discouraging ones.

Praise and thank God for everything in your life. In advance, give heartfelt thanks for the good you desire in the future.

• A THANKFUL HEART WILL PUT YOUR VALUES AND PRIORITIES INTO RIGHT PERSPECTIVE. We're all familiar with the story of the man who complained because he had no shoes until he met a man who had no feet. We think we are not as fortunate as someone else. We look at the lives and accomplishments of others with envy, which in turn closes the channels through which our own good could come to us. A feeling of gratitude helps us to sort out the really important issues of life from those that are transient and fleeting.

A newspaper reporter wrote this after the death of his wife: "We think our loved ones are going to live forever and we put off saying the really important things to them. If only I could look into Kathy's eyes and tell her how much she means to me. . . I can't do that now, and it seems the only thing I can do is to try to make other people know what they have. Look at your wife, your husband, your children, your parents, your friends. If you think you have things pretty nice, say it out loud. Don't assume that they are going to be there forever. It is too late for me, but maybe it isn't for you."

A great preacher of another era wrote this marvelous little piece of wisdom about the magnetic power of thankfulness:

"If one should give me a dish of sand and tell me that there are particles of iron in it, I might look for those particles with my eyes, and search for them with my clumsy fingers, and be unable to detect them; but let me take a magnet and sweep through the sand and now it would instantly draw to itself the almost invisible particles, by the mere power of attraction. The unthankful heart, like my finger, discovers no mercies, but let the thankful heart sweep through the day, and as the magnet finds the iron, so will the thankful heart, in every hour, find some heavenly blessings, only the iron in God's sand is pure gold!"

[November 1994]

IGNITING HOLY-DAY SPIRIT

"I suggest three ways in which we can recapture, or find for the first time, the true spirit of this holiday season."

A little girl stayed behind in the place of worship when her mother left with friends. When the child finally joined her mother outside, she was asked. "What were you doing in there all by yourself after the service ended?" To which the little girl replied, "Nothing . . . I was just loving God."

This is the season for love--love for God and love for each other. It is about music, giving, sights, sounds, tastes, feelings, joy and laughter, but above all it is about love.

For some, this is a season of irritation, frustration, tired feet and frazzled nerves. Ours is an age of noise, rushing about, and instant everything. There is a beautiful contrast between light and noise. Watch the sun rising in the east, quietly stealing into the sky, dispelling the darkness, gently waking all nature to life and loveliness. It doesn't shout. It moves silently across the world, transforming it. So it is with the year-end spirit, which is a deep, inner joy and awareness, a feeling of grateful humility and wonder that we can rise to new spiritual heights, not by pouring over self-help books, but by quietly sitting in communion with the holiness of our own being.

I suggest three ways in which we can re-capture, or find for the first time, the true spirit of this holiday season. They are qualities or ingredients of that magical night when love was born in an all-inclusive way.

A feeling of expectancy. Watch children as the holidays approach, or remember your own childhood feelings--the excitement and suspension and wonder. Where is your expectancy today? Hopefully, not with the things you'll get, but rather, with the beauty and richness you will experience and share with others during the season.

Many have missed the real spirit of this time because they have lost the sense of expectancy, and cannot find it by efforts put into the outer preparations, no matter how frantically they try to manufacture it.

Secondly, the spirit of year-end is irrevocably bound to the spirit of love. Do you have love in your heart today? Do you love yourself for the wonderful expression of God that you are? Of course you love your family members and friends. That's easy, but what about the people who may have caused you pain or unhappiness? Can you love the person while perhaps disliking the deed that caused you suffering? That's called unconditional love. That kind of love is not easy to experience, but it is the unmistakable evidence of the holiday spirit.

Why hasn't this time of year lost its magic, its power to change lives? I think it is because we need to hear the good news over and over, year after year. We need to be reminded of God's great love, to know that we are never beyond his love and its power to transform our lives.

A man shopping in an antique store noticed on a back shelf, buried among cracked dishes and worn ornaments, the figurine of an angel and a little boy. The statuette was crusted with grime and soot, but the man saw something other shoppers had missed. As he held it in his hand, he said to himself, "This must have been lovely at one time. I'll restore it and use it in our decorations this year." He bought the figurine and hurried home to begin the restoration. In his workshop he painted the angel and the child with pure white paint, then touched the angel's wings and the child's hair with sparkling gold paint. Every stroke of his brush worked new magic, as the dirty, neglected piece was transformed before his eyes. As he held the new creation proudly in his hands, he thought, "Isn't this what happens every December? We come to the end of the year, weary, tarnished from the wear and tear of daily living, and the holidays call us once more to uncover the angel nature which lies beneath all the dust and grime. It was there all the time. We are restored with the awareness of who we really are."

The third element in experiencing the spirit of the holiday is joy. The angel in us seems to be revealed more fully every time we laugh, rejoice, think joyful thoughts. A French writer wrote this: " The most wasted day of all is that in which you have not laughed." We can take the light touch into our holiday preparations as we remember that we have an inner reserve greater than any demands we might make upon it. We can "let the government be upon His shoulders" and enjoy the season as never before.

The message is that if enough of us will practice expectancy of good, increase our flow of love out into the world and the light touch as we go about our many extra tasks, and deeply feel the inner joy of the season, we can change the atmosphere of a family, a nation, a world.

Will you join me in letting the holiday spirit take over in your life, not just for this special time of year, but all year long? Then, on January 1st, we won't have to ask, "Where did the glow go?"

GOD BLESS YOU WITH A WONDERFUL HOLIDAY!

[December 1994]

BE REALLY ALIVE IN '95!

A few days ago I was out walking along a dirt path near my home. I found my thoughts going ahead to the new year nearly upon us. Then my attention was drawn to the cloudless sky where a sky-writer was etching a message . . . HAPPY 1995.

I found myself asking this question: Am I getting my New Year's message from the ground, the dirt under my feet, or from the sky? I decided at that moment to look up instead of down this year. When there are problems and challenges, instead of wallowing in all the details, the complications, I will look up and seek to find the inspiration and guidance that always comes when we take our mind off the problem and put it on God.

Your life, and the lives of those around you, is largely determined by the way you think and react to what happens to you. Won't you join me this year in making a serious commitment to the idea that we are going to have a truly great year? We habitually go around saying to the people we meet, HAPPY NEW YEAR, but that greeting is superficial unless we become new persons, unless we are willing to drop old hang-ups, excuses, conflicts, and negativity, for new motivation and purpose.

Remember the statement that what mind can conceive, man/woman can achieve. Won't you give attention to looking up, getting a new vision of what life can be, seeing it grow more beautiful every day? Norman Cousins wrote: "The tragedy of life is not death, but rather what we allow to die in us while we live." The beginning of a new year is the ideal time to put into practice all the truths we know, all the good ideas that we've put on the shelf.

Many years ago, I saved a sum of money for some highly touted Miracle Face Cream. Directions said to apply it twice a day, let it dry, then wash it off. After the first few days, failing to detect any miraculous improvement, I put it back on the shelf and forgot about it until I did my annual house cleaning. Of course there was no miracle for me. I didn't use the product correctly, or give it a chance. Haven't you had one or more good ideas that you strongly felt were going to improve your life--perhaps an exercise routine, a commitment to read more good books, a determination to overcome some negative habit? Then you got a bit lazy, and gradually the excitement of the new idea faded away. The following suggestions have helped to motivate and keep me going in new, improved directions for many years. . .

• BE WILLING TO GIVE UP THE ATTITUDES, FEARS, AND OUTWORN BELIEVES THAT HAVE LIMITED YOU. Do you think you have to be sick just because there is an epidemic going around? Are you convinced that the economy determines your financial well-being? Such beliefs are untrue and limiting. Get rid of them!

• PAY ATTENTION TO YOUR HEALTH. Be willing to pay the price for good health with exercise, recreation, quality foods, and positive ideas. Don't overlook the mind-body connection.

• PUT YOURSELF ON A HEALTHY MENTAL DIET. How long has it been since you read a stimulating book, one that lifted your spirits, or taken a class that stretched and challenged your thinking?

• DECIDE TO BE A MORE AWARE PERSON IN 1995. Work to develop a keener awareness of things you would ordinarily overlook--a sense of wonder in nature, a greater appreciation of the intangible but very real presence of love all around you. Consider what Marcus Bach termed "serendipity," the ability to find adventure in the most commonplace of events.

A young man was delivering a cord of wood to our little cottage. While he unloaded the wood, we had a lively conversation. I learned all about his life. Later that night, looking back and reviewing my day, as I do every night, I realized what a pleasurable experience I would have missed had I just called out, "Put the wood beside the storage shed." Awareness is the antenna of the soul, out to pick up more and more opportunities for sharing and lifting another human being.

• FINALLY, FALL IN LOVE. Do you remember when you first fell in love? It makes no difference whether it was 60 years ago or yesterday, you can recall the headiness, the lightness, the feeling that everything was right in your world. What would happen in our lives, our relationships, our businesses, every aspect of our lives, if we really turned on to love, if we allowed ourselves to be captured again by that greatest of all emotions?

Do you feel that you have no one to love? Not so! The world is crying out for it. The person sitting beside you in a theater, or in church, or on the bus, might be hungry for a sincere smile.

In a class one time, a man responded to this suggestion with the words, "But I am just naturally reserved. I can't reach out and take someone's hand." I reminded him that the word "reserved" means to keep back, to save up for future use, and I continued, "If this is your feeling, what are you saving your warm, loving response for?"

There is no time like the present to begin to let your lovability blossom. There is no limit to the supply. The more love you allow to flow through you, the more you will have to enrich your own life.

Three months later I performed the marriage ceremony for this shy man and the equally shy woman whose hand he reached for that day!

[January 1995]

WAYS TO SAY, 'I LOVE YOU'

A French writer once wrote, "The supreme grace is to love ourselves." Does that sound immature and egotistical? On the surface, perhaps, but we seldom realize that only those who have a secure knowledge of self and a sense of personal dignity can share with others, and dare to love. An article in a recent parenting magazine stated that before the average child finishes elementary school, he or she has heard thousands of "cant's" . . . "no's" . . . "never's" . . . "shut-up's" . . . "don't be stupid's" and other damaging, devaluing words. It is no wonder that so many people grow up believing that the world is a terrible, strange place.

Dr. William Glasser, in his book Reality Therapy, says this: "At all times in our lives we must have at least one person who cares about us and for whom we care. If we do not have this essential person, we will not be able to fulfill our basic needs."

In an old cartoon, "Marvin" the baby cartoon character watches his mother water her plants carefully and tenderly, and he thinks, "Mom spends so much time with her plants, she forgets about me. Doesn't she know that babies wilt, too?" Respect for the self is like handling a delicate plant. The self needs nurturing and attention. None of us is sure of ourselves all of the time, and we need the support of others who aren't so close to our problems, who can affirm our self worth and bring out the best in us.

How can we be empowering in the lives of those around us and at the same time nourish and feed ourselves? First we must forgive. It is the only way to heal hard feelings, guilt, and poor self-image. The story is told of a Catholic priest in a small Philippine village. He was well-liked by the people but he suffered such guilt over some sin he had committed early in his seminary training that, although he served his people faithfully, there was never a sense of peace, no feeling of God's forgiveness. A young woman in his parish claimed to have visions in which she spoke with Christ and he with her. In an effort to test the validity of her visions, the priest asked her to ask Christ what sin he, the priest, had committed years earlier. When the woman came back, she said she had done as the priest had asked, and the priest said impatiently, "Well, what did he say? to which the woman answered, "He said, "I don't remember." Forgiveness says, "I love you."

Another way to express our love is by listening. A sixteen year old girl told her school counselor, "When my parents hear me out and don't interrupt with 'Oh, no, you can't do that,' then I can really talk to them." Try giving the simple gift of listening and attention to someone and watch that person blossom and bloom.

Closely behind listening is the gift of patience. A constant state of impatience and irritability conveys the unspoken message, "You are not important to me." A youngster on the bus was asking questions non-stop, of his mother. Exasperated, she lashed out, "Shut up!" Hesitantly, the boy tugged at his mother's sleeve and said, "Mommy, it's me, Danny!"

Another mother was constantly interrupted in her housework by a curious three-year old, who kept calling her to the garden to see a butterfly, or an ant, or a flower. A friend who was visiting was amazed at the mother's patience and asked, "Don't you ever just want to scream?' The smiling mother answered, "Well, I brought her into the world. The least I can do is let her show it to me."

We can show our love by giving "quality time." This hackneyed phrase is often used as an excuse for giving very little time. St. Paul wrote, "All the special gifts and powers from God will some day come to an end, but love goes on forever." I'm sure that many of you treasure, as I do, children and grandchildren who are growing up too fast. No one can measure the positive effect your loving influence will have on their lives, and the bonus that it brings to you, right in the moment and in precious memories.

A small girl was adopted into a loving family and one night, after the father had read her her bedtime story, she hugged him harder and longer than usual. When she finally took her arms from around his neck, she looked into his eyes and said, "Daddy, is this what heaven will be like?"

We say "I love you" when we affirm the worth of another person. Being affirmative does not mean overlooking faults and mistakes, but it does mean separating the doer from the deed, loving the essential goodness of the person, expecting the best, looking for the good. It isn't enough to mouth the words, "I love you." Those words, without supporting action, are as dead as faith without works.

Won't you join me in seeing miracles in relationships, health, and conditions around our world, as together, we FORGIVE . . . LISTEN . . . ARE PATIENT . . . GIVE TIME . . . ARE GENTLE . . . AND TENDER . . . AND AFFIRM . . . AND SUPPORT?

Ann Landers wrote in her column: "Love is friendship that has caught fire. It is quiet understanding, mutual confidence, sharing and forgiving. It is loyalty through good times and bad times. It settles for less than perfection, and makes allowances for human weaknesses. Love is content with the present. It hopes for the future, but doesn't brood over the past. If you have love in your life, it can make up for a great many things you lack. If you don't have love, no matter what else there is, it is not enough."

[February 1995]

THE TURNING POINT TRUTHS

Do you remember a time when life was somewhat predictable, a time when you could count on certain conditions--a good education, a happy family life, reasonably good health--all the components of the "good" life? And have you noticed recently that very few people, including yourself, seem to be facing a certain future, that plans are interrupted by ill health, changes in relationships, unseen and unwelcome events that leave one with very little sense of control over one's life?

My friends, join the club. Most of your friends are members, coping with changes they did not ask for or anticipate. As a charter member of the club, please allow me to share with you some truths I have gleaned from my Turning Points, in the hope that they will encourage you to face your own challenges with confidence and assurance. Someone sent me this bit of wisdom by Jean Platt: "How frail our trust--how fragile our belief--how frequently that happening construed as tragedy becomes, in retrospect, a blessing when examined and reviewed. How rare the heart that ponders and perceives what is hidden in the burden it receives."

This call to awareness, added to Aristotle's observation that "the unexamined life is not worth living," plus Dr. Bernie Siegel's comforting statement that "turning points in our lives are to be welcomed, indications that we have stayed in one place long enough and that life has something new and different, even better to offer." . . . All of these started me on a quest to find the blessing in disappointment, cancer, loss of a familiar and loved career. AND I HAVE FOUND THE GIFT!

Again quoting Dr. Siegel . . ."Getting rid of the disease or the problem is not the main issue. The goal is peace of mind."

Oliver Wendell Holmes once said, "A mind stretched by a new idea can never return to its original dimension." So my first step in finding the hidden blessing was to acknowledge the problem, face it squarely and head-on, and then to ask for answers about how to deal with it constructively. That took me to the next phase of my healing and peace of mind, that of deepening my connection with God. You need not be religious or subscribe to any particular form of religion . . . simply accept the possibility that you just may be a spiritual being, living in a physical world which allows you to have challenges in order to grow and recognize your innate divinity. That is part of the gift--the incredible feeling of oneness with everything and everyone.

Such departure from one's usual and limited concepts about life can be unsettling, and this stretching requires courage, the willingness to step out into the unknown, secure in the knowledge that the divinity within you is always on your side, urging you on to greater creativity, more expanded living. Emerson is one of my favorite philosophers and this statement has carried me through many dark days: "The things I have seen teach me to trust the Creator for the things I have not seen."

Patience is another requisite for moving into your promised land. Be willing to trust a Higher intelligence that loves you and wants your best. Remember that God's delays are not God's denials. Alexander Graham Bell said, "When one door closes, another door always opens, but we often look so long and so regretfully upon the closed door that we don't see the one that has opened for us." I've discovered that this quality of patience is closely connected with expectancy--expecting the best, but living totally in the moment with all its blessings and beauties and possibilities.

A grandmother sent this poem to Dear Abby, saying that it had been written by her 14 year old grandson. Abby checked up on the grandmother's claim, met the boy, and was still astounded at such wisdom from one so young. The boy's poem is called . . .

"Present Tense"

It was spring, but it was summer I wanted,
    the warm days and the great outdoors.
It was summer, but it was fall I wanted,
    the colorful leaves and the cool, dry air.
It was fall, but it was winter I wanted,
    the beautiful snow and the joy of the holiday season.
It was winter, but it was spring I wanted,
    the warmth and the blossoming of nature.
I was a child, but it was adulthood I wanted,
    the freedom and the respect.
I was twenty, but it was thirty I wanted,
    the maturity and the sophistication.
I was middle aged, but it was twenty I wanted,
    the youth and the free spirit.
I was retired, but it was middle age I wanted,
    the presence of mind without the limitations.
My life was over, but I never got what I wanted!

Finally, my friend, as you come into a greater awareness of your connection with the Source [God, Life, the Force, Divine Energy] as you see ever more clearly the gift that your challenge is offering you, and are grateful for the growth and new maturity, try giving yourself away--in love of life, in service to others, in sharing the light that has come into your life. Service to others has a wonderful way of lifting us out of our own concerns. Someone needs exactly what you have to give, so open your eyes and your ears and your heart to LIFE, and give to others that which you have received so lavishly from the Source of all good.

God bless you.

[March 1995]

THE WAY OUT IS IN

Einstein once said that the most important question humankind must answer is this: "Is the universe a friendly place?" He suggested that the answer to this question affects all other thought and behavior on a personal and general level. How would you answer that question today, in the wake of recent tragic events, including the Oklahoma City bombing? Was your faith in a friendly universe shaken, or perhaps even destroyed? Where are you looking for answers? Are you reaching out to spiritual leaders, books, the media, hoping to find some sense and reason in these difficult days of disillusionment and heartache?

Four years ago, on the eve of major cancer surgery, I had a dream. There were two wheels before me and the hub of one wheel was terribly off center. As the wheel wobbled along, it was obvious that a ride over such a faulty wheel would be a rough, uncertain one. The hub of the other wheel was perfectly centered, and it moved easily and smoothly over rough terrain. The message was clear. I went into surgery the next morning visualizing myself as this wheel, centered and poised in the knowledge that although the surgery would leave my body scarred and incomplete, physically, nothing could damage, destroy, or change in any way, the real self that I am. My recovery was a miracle to doctors and family and friends. It was complete, speedy, relatively painless, and the picture of the wheel has served me well ever since.

My belief system is built on the understanding and acceptance of the idea that life is eternal, that the true essence of individuals cannot be destroyed, only changed in form. I have found comfort in remembering this truth, knowing that those lost after dreadful events do live in another dimension and will be reunited with loved ones in God's own time and way. There is no way, of course, to bring instant comfort and reassurance to those who have lost loved ones. Time will bring a measure of peace and acceptance, however there is something that all of us can do to speed the healing process for those who grieve in a personal way, and for all of us who share their pain.

Emerson said: "The things I have seen teach me to trust the Creator for the things I have not seen." My friend, look back over your life and note the times you have been brought through some difficult experience, a time, perhaps, when you seem to have been delivered from a dreadful happening. Whatever your religious or philosophical belief, if it is even a tiny, vague hope in something beyond the pain and uncertainty of the present, nourish that fragile sprout. The way out of discouragement and fear is to turn within, to whatever spiritual roots you have, and to find there, at the center of your being, a calmness, a certainty that defies words, but which is real and which meets your needs, at all levels.

A college student shared with me last week his feelings of frustration, and confusion, his disillusionment with the idea of a friendly universe. He said, "I just can't believe in a God who would let such a [bombing] take place--where is the God of love and compassion we're supposed to trust?" His pain and confusion were clearly visible in his eyes and in his shaking voice.

Platitudes can be empty and even offensive at times, and in this case totally inappropriate, so I simply shared with him a belief which has sustained me throughout my long life--the acceptance that we are created in the image and likeness of a God of love, inheriting God-like attributes, but that also, as human beings, we are given the power of free will, the ability to choose how we will see ourselves and our world. If we choose to use our God-like qualities of love and compassion and kindness, we not only enrich our own lives, but the consciousness of the human race is lifted. However if we use the power of choice for selfish, evil acts, we will ultimately reap the unhappy results, and our world will suffer.

I suggested to my young friend that we try to be part of the solution, not part of the problem, by practicing the following steps each day . . . to spend time in nature, feeling our oneness with it, loving the earth, the sky, the rivers, the animals, and all other human beings. [In loving, we do not have to like the deeds performed by others, but we must love the spiritual essence of them, as we love ourselves]. Take a few moments to be silent, seeing yourself as the stable wheel, certain in your understanding that you are a spiritual being and cannot die. Live in the moment, alert to opportunities to help others find their quiet center, not by words but by example. Give more attention to being instead of so much attention to doing. Finally, from your own peaceful center, free from judgment, un-forgiveness and condemnation, send your love and blessings out into the world. As you hear of bad news, watch the graphic scenes on TV, see yourself as a broadcasting station for healing and wholeness. You are not denying facts, you are acting as an agent for restoration, balance, and saneness.

Dear friend, you and I can make a difference for good, not only in this latest emergency, but for all time, as we recognize that the way out of our pain and suffering, is to go within, to the Source of all help, and then to share that realization with our world.

God bless you!

[June 1995]

BOUNTY'S BOOMERANG

"The Great Law: Everything you think, say, or do comes back to you."

Everything you say, think, and do, is subject to the law of compensation. Emmet Fox wrote in The Sermon on the Mount (Matthew 5) that in five short verses we are given the most staggering document ever presented to mankind.

We are told more about the nature of humanity, the meaning of life, the importance of conduct and the art of living, the secret of happiness and success, the way out of trouble, the approach to God, the emancipation of the soul and the salvation of the world, than all the philosophers and theologians put together have told us, for it explains the great law, which is: EVERYTHING YOU THINK, SAY, AND DO, COMES BACK TO YOU. This law is based on the truth that "Whatsoever a person soweth, that also shall he reap."

Whatever you give, you receive. If you wish for others to have good luck, good luck will eventually come to you. If you try to cheat someone, criticize, or lie, be assured that somewhere along the line, you will be the recipient of the same treatment. It is the precise cosmic law of sowing and reaping. And if you love others, you will be loved in return.

Actually this law is very comforting and dependable in a world which seems so unfair at times. Who of us has not questioned, "How can he get away with that kind of action? Why should this terrible thing happen to me when I haven't done a harmful thing to anyone?"

Listen to these words of Emerson: "Justice is not postponed. The dice of God are always loaded. The world looks like a multiplication table, or mathematical equation, which, turn it as you will, balances itself. Every secret is told, every crime punished, every virtue rewarded, every wrong redressed, in silence and certainty."

If this simple truth were fully understood, there would be no more wars or crime or unhappiness. Emmet Fox continued: "If a person could for a single second, really understand the meaning of the words, "Judge not that you be not judged," his whole life would be revolutionized."

An ancient legend tells of a woman who baked three loaves every day, for a wealthy family, her own family, and one loaf for charity. Each day as she placed the charity loaf on her window sill, for whoever would take it, she prayed for the safe return of her son who had gone abroad to seek his fortune. Every day the charity loaf was snatched off the shelf by a crazy little hunchbacked man, who irritated the woman, for instead of expressing gratitude for the food, persistently spat out this odd remark, "The evil you do stays with you. The good you do comes back to you."

After months of listening to this weird little man and his constant repetition of the strange words in his unpleasant, crackling voice, the woman decided to put a stop to his unwelcome visits. That day she put into the charity bread a lethal dose of poison. But as she pulled the loaf from the oven, she was horrified to think what she had done, so she threw the poisoned load into the fire and substituted one of her family's loaves. Later that morning the little man took the loaf, muttering his usual remark. The woman watched, still shaking from what she had almost done. That evening there was a knock on her door, and there stood her son, gaunt from hunger, clothes tattered and torn. She threw her arms around him and held him tightly as he said, "Mother, it is a miracle that I am here. About a mile from here I began to faint from hunger and actually fell by the road. I hadn't had a mouthful of food for four days, then a little old hunchback man came by, eating a loaf of bread, and when he saw my condition, he gave me the whole loaf." The mother turned white and leaned against the table for support, as she remembered the words of the annoying beggar, "The evil you do stays with you. The good you do comes back to you."

I will never forget a young man who was in my group, as we toured the Soviet Union ten years ago. One night, in the home of a Russian family in Moscow, I "caught" him in the act of placing rubles in a drawer in the kitchen, to be found later by surprised and delighted Russian hosts. I watched him closely from then on, and saw him repeat this anonymous act of generosity over and over. Sitting beside him an a bus one day, I confessed that I had witnessed his kindness, and asked why he did what he did. With a wide grin, he told me that he got so much pleasure out of his actions, and that he had learned a long time ago, through his mother's example, that such giving was the sure way to ensure his own well-being and success. He added, "And besides, it is so much fun to see people surprised and pleased!"

If you are feeling a bit pinched, emotionally or financially, if your health is not what you would wish, start to give, with no thought of return, no strings attached. Your good, cast out into the world, will come back to you, in whatever form you need that good. It is a law.

[July 1995]

THE ART OF VACATIONING

I am convinced that vacationing is an art, just as important as managing one's money, getting along with people, and accomplishing one's goals. Vacationing should be as individual as our tastes in food or clothing. Of course, when one's vacation is taken with others, family members or friends, it is necessary to take into consideration the likes and dislikes of others.

The first step in successful vacationing is to ask yourself, "What do I really want from my vacation? Do I want new sights and new faces, excitement, lots of fun, or do I want to spend time alone, renewing myself in mind and body?" Even if your plans include others, and there is the need to compromise at times, please recognize the importance of having some time to yourself, being good to you.

One of the first things you will consider in planning a vacation is what equipment to take [including appropriate clothes, camping gear, books, etc.] but even more important than the right material equipment is a right attitude toward the whole experience. Then you will be realistic in your goals for a vacation. If you are a conservative person by nature, if your idea of the perfect vacation is going out into your own backyard with a good book and hours of empty time ahead of you, by all means don't choose for your vacation a week in an expensive resort where every moment you are conscious of how much you are spending. A postcard received from a man in this situation simply said, "Having a wonderful time. Wish I could afford it."

Another consideration is to travel lightly. This is advice I always wished I'd followed when carrying my own luggage farther than expected. The idea to keep in mind when packing is Keep It Simple.

• TRAVEL EXPECTANTLY. Expect your vacation to be full of wonderful surprises. Robert Louis Stevenson said "To travel hopefully is better than to arrive." I have frequently remarked that in all the trips I have taken in the last 25 years, I have enjoyed each trip at least three times: Looking forward to it, the trip itself, and the happy memories of it.

• TRAVEL HUMBLY. Remember that when you visit other people, you are the visitor. They may speak and act in ways that are foreign to you, but the art of vacationing includes learning to treat people and places with respect for their traditions and customs. When we travel humbly, knowing that in every person, every contact, every experience, there is something for us to learn, the whole vacation experience can be incredibly rewarding and enriching.

• TRAVEL COURTEOUSLY AND GRATEFULLY. One friend who has had years of successful vacationing makes it a practice, on arriving in a strange country, to learn two words immediately. They are "Thank you." He invariably gets red carpet treatment.

• TRAVEL WITH AN OPEN MIND, CURIOSITY AND IMAGINATION. Leave your prejudices at home. It is not how far you go, but how deep you go. Remember that Thoreau wrote a big book about tiny Walden Pond. A Spanish proverb says, "He who would bring home the wealth of the Indies, must carry the wealth of the Indies with him." Be flexible. So you miss your plane. There may be a very good reason for the delay. Look for adventure in detours and delays. Some of my most exciting experiences have come about because of a re-arrangement of plans.

• TRAVEL CONFIDENTLY. Remember that people are basically the same, the world over. We may have differently colored skin, unusual customs [in our eyes] but we all have the same underlying hopes and dreams and desires.

• TRAVEL RELAXED. Make up your mind that you are going to have a glorious time. Remember that the most important thing you take with you is your awareness that God is with you, making all arrangements, planning surprises and adventures that can only come about when you allow God to be in charge. For years I have used the following affirmation before starting on any vacation, whether around the world, or just a quiet stay-at-home retreat. "I live and move in the safety of God's presence at all times, in all places. Divine order governs my whole vacation, including right plans, right places, right prices and right companions. I let God's love shine through me to bless all with whom I come in contact. Thank you, God."

When you return to your home the pressure may begin to build up again. It will be a challenge not to fall back into the old routine as if you had never had a time of refreshment and change of pace. Don't let that happen to you! Sit back in your chair and remember how it felt to lean up against the sturdy trunk of a tree. Mentally take yourself back to the forest, or to the congenial group of friends with whom you shared some wonderful times--wherever you found peace. Go through it all again, every bit of it. Bring it to mind whenever you feel the need for the peace and joy and relaxation you experienced.

I have loved the following "Vacation Prayer" by Elizabeth Searle Lamb. "God bless all vacationers. God bless all who vacation at home. Let this be a time of rich meaning, a time of rest and renewal. Let it bring peace to mind and soul. God bless all who sail in sunny waters, climb snow-capped peaks, sun on sandy shores, or ride wilderness trails. Surround them with your protecting presence, fill them with your life and strength and joy. God bless all who travel in strange lands. Let them see you in greeting smiles, let them hear your voice in words of familiar accent or foreign tongue. Let their ways be made smooth and happy and free from worry and care. Open their eyes to the beauty all around them, open their mind to Truth everywhere, open their hearts to your enfolding love."

[August 1995]

A SAVING SENSE OF HUMOR

"Laughter ranks as the supreme wonder drug."
For too many people, there seems to be a belief that if you are going to be good, you can't have any fun, that to be religious is to be serious all the time. As one writer observed, "These joyless religionists have just enough religion to make them feel miserable. They have never entered into the legacy that Christ has promised, "I have come that my joy may be in you, and that your joy may be full." I would like to explore with you some very practical reasons why joy and laughter ought to be an integral part of our lives, every day.

Dr. Ernest Campbell, a prominent New York minister whose congregations were treated weekly to a healthy dose of laughter, said this, "A sense of humor is one of the signs of a healthy life. One of the surest indications of a sick and mentally disturbed personality is the inability to laugh." Our most popular medical authorities are telling us that laughter has therapeutic value. Behavioral scientists have found, in exhaustive experiments, that when it comes to promoting mental and physical health, and actually prolonging human life, laugher ranks as the supreme wonder drug. They tell us that laughter has a profound and almost instantaneous effect on virtually ever important organ in the body, as well as on the glands and the entire nervous system.

I have always sprinkled my talks and sermons liberally with appropriate humor, and am in the process now of putting many of the more well-received stories into a book. A few of my favorites, with the hope that they will brighten up YOUR day . . .

A Minister in Georgia was driving a friend out to show the friend his old home. After several miles of winding, dusty roads, the friend remarked, "You had to be called by the Lord. He was the only one who could find you."

A Methodist minister in Phoenix telephoned the editor of a local newspaper and said, "I want to thank you for the error made in the story announcing my Sunday service." The editor gulped and asked why the minister was pleased if the story had been incorrect. The pastor answered, "My sermon subject was 'What Jesus saw in a publican,' but the newspaper story read, 'What Jesus saw in a Republican,' and I had the biggest audience I've had in months!"

One authority had this to say, "Laughter is the healer of the body and of the mind. If people would laugh more they could actually laugh off many of the minor mental and physical ills that plague them. In addition to the fact that laughter is frequently the best medicine, it has three notable advantages: It is by far more pleasant to take . . . you don't have to worry about getting an overdose . . . it doesn't cost anything and you don't have to see an expensive specialist to get a prescription.

Humor not only saves us from ulcers, heart attacks and other maladies that result from too much tension, it also saves us from ourselves. Without a healthy sense of humor we take ourselves too seriously. When the ego gets blown up out of all reasonable proportion, someone is sure to come along and deflate us with a barb of humor.

One of the most familiar examples of humor and laughter is to be found in the book of Genesis. You may remember that when God announced to the aged Abraham that he was going to be a father, Abraham fell down on his face and laughed. It was unthinkable that he and his wife Sarah, at their advanced age, should become parents. They were not willing to accept the strangeness, the far-out quality of God's grace. They said, "This just cannot be!" They saw only the impossible side of God's statement. After the amazing birth, however, Sarah recognized the foolishness of her laughter of unbelief. She not only received the gift of a precious son, but also the amazing gift of joy. A new kind of laughter was born, and in naming her son Isaac, which means, "laughter," Sarah exclaims, "God has made laughter for me. All who hear about this shall rejoice with me."

Finally [and someone has said that the true optimist is the woman who puts her shoes back on when the Minster says, "finally"], after we have recognized the value of laughter in healing our physical and mental woes, after we have realized the role of joy and laughter in keeping us flexible and humble, after we have experienced the saving grace of a sense of humor, we come to the conclusion that the person who gives humor a large part in his life, who has learned to laugh, has also learned to trust the Universe [God, the Force, whatever your name for a Higher Power] and to let that Power carry his burdens and sorrows and challenges. Such a person has learned to travel light, to release the burdens of the day at the close of every day, to give up grudges and un-forgiveness, to trust a benevolent Universe to bring him through the ups and downs of human life safely and surely. In the midst of fear, unrest, revolution, tragedy, he can live in peace believing that there is a great divine event toward which all creation moves, as Emerson expressed it. Such a person does all in his/her power to help others, to make a difference in his/her community, to share what light she/he has with those who struggle and get discouraged, but she/he does it with a sure, unshakable faith that the eternal values can never fail.

[September 1995]

A SEASON FOR EVERYTHING

"Could it be that some of the painful frustrations and feelings of unrest in our lives are caused by our ignorance of natural rhythms and our unwillingness to flow with them?"

We traditionally think of the fall season as a time of new beginnings. At the same time, in nature we observe the process of letting go. Trees drop their leaves, certain animals go to sleep for the winter. All nature functions according to dependable cycles, beginnings and endings.

Since human beings are part of the universal cycle of natural progression, could it be that some of the painful frustrations and feelings of unrest in our lives are caused by our ignorance of these natural rhythms and our unwillingness to flow with them?

A short time ago I moved into a new home in the peaceful foothills of Ashland. I hope it will be my home for the "duration" and, in preparation for the move, I did a lot of sorting and discarding. There was one box of favorite garments that I simply haven't had the heart to give up--the elegant lace gown I had made for my daughter's wedding--a lovely wool suit, purchased in Scotland 20 years ago-- a very expensive blouse, a gift from my husband when I was several sizes smaller than I am today. For years I have packed and unpacked them all, reasoning that some day I'd be a size 10 again and have occasion to wear them.

One day last fall, watching the fading leaves fall from the magnificent trees in Lithia park, I saw the possible answer to my human reluctance to let go. I realized that trees don't hang onto their leaves when those leaves have served their purpose in providing shade and beauty through the hot summer months. It is as if the tree instinctively knows that there can be no new growth in the spring unless the old leaves give space on the branches. So the leaves are freed from their attachment to the branch at just the right time, in a silent mutual agreement between the tree and the leaf. The leaves fall to earth to become part of the rich soil which will nurture the tree as it gets ready to bring forth the new spring growth.

The lesson was clear and simple. I had been praying for newness in my life, while being unwilling to let go of the old. Why hadn't I accepted the fact that those cherished pieces of clothing had served their purpose? Was my reluctance caused by the doubt that there would not be comparable garments in the future which would bring me joy and sentimental value? Would I ever know if I clung tenaciously to the old treasures, dear as they were?

That very day I went through my special boxes and wrapped each piece of clothing lovingly in tissue paper. I thought of several friends who had admired the various articles and might yet get some joy from wearing them. What really amazed me was the feeling of freedom and lightness that came over me as I distributed my "gems" to surprised and appreciative friends.

Now there is no more guilt over the fact that I can no longer fit into those things--no more false, unrealistic expectations that I might someday get into a size 10. As my letting go adventure continues, I am extending it to no-longer useful ideas, beliefs, assumptions that were right and appropriate for another time and place. It is now time to release and replace them with a new philosophy, more compatible with my current, more relaxed life style, and oh, how sweet it is!

Now I see many other applications of this principle of cherishing the moment, seeing the value of delays and seeming obstacles. My father helped me throughout a long and painful bout with a crippling bone disease which had its onset when I was 10, and carried over until my mid-20's. His constant advice was: "Honey, grasp the moment. Your mind is not affected by the fact that you can't walk. Make the most of this time of physical inactivity. Use your imagination to visualize the life you want. Don't give up. Use this time wisely, and someday you'll be surprised to see how this experience has prepared you for what you came to do." Now I know that I listened to my father, and how grateful I am for his loving counsel. I learned to type, and to read and comprehend very quickly. In my years in the ministry, I would have been lost without these skills. Now I see that those seemingly "lost" years were a valuable part of my life plan and, when the purpose of that experience was complete, I was able to walk and continue a normal life.

Miracles began to happen in my life. There was more order, more love, more understanding of the reason for certain conditions and relationships. You see, my friend, you are wishing for everyone in your life what you are wishing for yourself--their highest good. You, and they, will be able to move through he cycles of life as normally and effortlessly as the leaves drop from the trees.

God bless!

[October 1995]

EVERYDAY GRACIOUSNESS

"Why do we need periodic reminders of the need for appreciation--not only for our own benefit, but for the good of others?"

Have you ever wondered why the spirit of thanksgiving and gratitude should be reserved for just one day out of the whole year? Why do we need periodic reminders of the need for appreciation--not only for our own benefit, but for the good of others?

Ian MacLaren, an author whose stories have charmed many of us for years, tells of an incident that had a tremendous impact on his life. He noticed a man feeling his way along the sidewalk with a white cane on a quiet residential street, running his hand carefully over the gates until he found the one he wanted. The man opened the gate and moved toward the door of what was apparently his home. As he reached the top step, he turned, and with simple dignity and grace, tipped his hat. MacLaren was puzzled; there was no one close for the man to tip his hat to, and besides, he was blind.

Stepping up to the man on the steps, he said, "Forgive my curiosity, my friend. I see that you are blind, and there is no one around, and yet you tipped your hat. May I ask who it is that you were saluting?"

"Oh, yes," replied the man. "I am tipping my hat to the universe." MacLaren said later that this simple act was like an act of worship, a salute of appreciation, an expression of gratitude for the wonder and beauty and goodness of life itself. What an inspiration it is to know someone like MacLaren's blind friend, someone who may, on the surface, have every reason to complain and be bitter about some affliction, but who, instead, revels in the adventure of life, grateful for the privilege of enjoying every day blessings.

One of my most loved teachers was a 90 year old woman who never preached a sermon--from a pulpit--but who practiced thanksgiving every moment of her life. Just what were her blessings? Food, shelter, a friendly fire, a few staunch friends, a host of memories, her unseen spiritual companions, the joy of a simple faith that had been tried and tested throughout a lifetime of adversity and challenges. But this friend had learned a powerful and effective secret for living her life to the fullest. She believed that instead of setting aside one day of the year as Thanksgiving Day, the practice should be reversed, that it made more sense to make 364 days in a year Thanksgiving Day, and set apart the one remaining day as "grouch day."

On that day, this wise woman suggested that everyone be free to air his or her grievances against life and the world. It would be a dismal day, she said, for those who have no sense of humor, but it would do people good to blow off steam, do their grumbling and complaining and then have it behind them. That would leave 364 days to fill with thanksgiving and praise for the blessings that we are usually too busy to notice when we are looking for all the things that might be wrong; I liked this idea, and accepted it for my own use. I chose a plain old Monday for this indulgence of finding fault but to my surprise, that day turned out to be the best of that whole week! There were unexpected phone calls from out-of-town friends, some exciting news in a letter, the day was filled with warm sunshine and puffy white clouds. Who could be grouchy on such a day?

The greatest collection of thanksgiving literature in the world, the Book of Psalms in the Bible, was produced by a people who had very few reasons for gratitude. Yet, in their miserable years of exile, above their laments beside the waters of Babylon, rose songs of praise to God, whom they continued to trust and thank for His goodness to them. These ancient Hebrews put into practice the theory of my 90 year old friend. Thanksgiving to God was not a special day with them, it was a daily experience, regardless of the circumstances of their lives.

I do not know what the 4th Thursday of November

means to you, but to me it means not only a personal silent expression of gratitude, but an awareness of the need to let love and appreciation be expressed in tangible ways-- inviting a lonely person to share our Thanksgiving feast- sending notes of appreciation to people we might be inclined to take for granted--support of a local organization providing food for the homeless. The ways are many, the need is great. The old phrase, "Put your money where your mouth is," might also mean, "Put some action into your good intentions and desire to help others."

Thanksgiving is a way, not just a day, and I believe that an expanded understanding of the real meaning of Thanksgiving, the willingness to extend oneself in the interests of others, and the practice of continual inner thankfulness can transform lives. May you and yours be blessed with the best Thanksgiving of your life!

[November 1995]

SAVORING THE SEASON'S SPIRIT

"Whatever your belief, my friend, I think you will admit that something happens at this time of year that defies description. People are kinder, more thoughtful, more forgiving. . ."

Every year about this time, I begin to search for new ways in which to experience anew the wonders and beauties of this holy season. With each passing year I realize more fully that Christmas is so much more than a day, more than the loved and familiar trappings we enjoy each year. It is more than a season, it is a spirit, a time to be reminded of the power of love and generosity and caring.

We may never know all the details concerning the great event of 2,000 years ago. There are those who believe that Jesus' birth was a myth, a pleasant folk tale around which people have constructed ceremonies and rituals and celebrations. Whatever your belief, my friend, I think you will admit that something happens at this time of year that defies description. People are kinder, more thought-ful, more forgiving. My belief includes the acceptance of the fact that something new did come into the world with the birth of Jesus--a wondrous energy that continues to affect the lives of all who accept it. That energy has been found in all great spiritual leaders, who spoke and taught the Truth, the oneness of all life, the spiritual identity of every living soul. In the world into which Jesus came there were countless laws pertaining to religious practice, but he brought a new law--the law of love, and those who live by that law find answers to their questions, peace of mind in a troubled world, and a purpose for living.

Someone once asked Mother Teresa, "Don't you ever become angry at the social injustices you see in India, or any of the places where you help the sick and dying?" Mother Teresa's response was, "Why should I expend energy in anger when I can expend it in love?"

I would like to suggest three simple lessons we can learn from the Christmas story.

• FIRST, to recognize that divine love can be translated into practical, everyday experiences. True, unconditional love is not a theory to be worshiped. It is a principle to be practiced.

• SECOND, to accept the fact that the same spiritual possibilities that Jesus demonstrated are in us. He claimed no special dispensation from God.

• THIRD, to see Christmas as a reminder each year that our individual consciousness can be transformed from attitudes of despair, apathy and fear, to attitudes of love, hope, and goodwill toward all people.

No matter what we may believe, personally, about the Christmas story, we can agree on the purpose of it, and we can see Christmas as a tremendous opportunity opened to us each year. We can find ways of using the outer symbols of Christmas in fresh and beautiful expressions. Every card, every decoration, every lovely carol, no matter how or where displayed, is an opportunity to unlock our hearts again, to give in to impulses to share our love, our supply of good things, our time and attention, in the true spirit of the season.

A little girl got a ball-point pen for Christmas and one day she drew a picture of a cat for her little brother, Jimmy. The little boy pointed out that the cat had no tail, to which she responded that the tail was still in the pen. Jimmy protested, "You can't put a cat's tail into a pen," to which his sister quickly replied, "Yes you can. Everything that comes out of a ball point pen, you have to think in first."

It is Christmas, the world over. The whole world is affected for good by that simple birth so long ago. Jesus lived for three decades, walking through the countryside in Palestine, and now, once a year his name is emblazoned in lights around the world. Because of his appearance on this earth, hearts at this time of year turn to deeds of kindness. Children breathe the very air in which miracles still take place. Millions of people rejoice. And millions of people continue to carry the message in their hearts and lives all year long. I have loved this bit of verse, and it has inspired me, year after year.

"The Work of Christmas"

When the song of the angels is stilled,
When the star in the sky is gone,
When the kings and princes are home,
When the shepherds are back with their flock,
The work of Christmas begins.
To find the lost,
To heal the broken,
To feed the hungry,
To release the prisoner,
To rebuild the nations,
To bring peace among brothers and sisters,
To make music in the heart!

Have a blessed, peaceful, love-filled Christmas, friends.

[December 1995]

LIFE IN A GIVING UNIVERSE

We need to be there for those who can benefit from our optimism and faith in a better world. . .

What do we really mean when we greet friends at this time of year with the familiar greeting, "Happy New Year?" Has it become such a cliché that we speak the words automatically, as if they are expected? I spent some time one year, really meditating on those words, my understanding of them, and their importance in our even casual relationships. I came to the conclusion that this is the real message behind the words, "I wish for you a year full of blessings, a year of freedom from everything which keeps you from expressing your infinite potential."

Now that you and I have put a away our 1995 calendars, let's think seriously about the fresh 12 months ahead. Do we look forward to some welcome changes in our lives . . . do we fully expect to make progress in our spiritual journey . . . do we really want to be free from the fears and insecurities and inhibitions that have limited us in the past? I once made a list of conditions from which I would like to be free -- do any items on my list sound familiar to you?

• FREEDOM FROM DEPENDENCY on people and conditions for my own peace of mind. How many times are we defeated by things around us -- the job we didn't get, the disapproval of someone important to us. Of course, people are important to us, but do we put too much responsibility on others to make us happy? Don Blanding once made a statement that became synonymous with his name: "Joy is an inside job." A full understanding of those words will free us from this first fear, for all time.

• FEAR OF THE FUTURE. A parishioner once sent me a Christmas card, listing all the things that had gone wrong in her life in just that one year - the list was long, loss of two loved ones, break down of her spouse, a house fire, death of her dog, etc., etc. She went on to say that she had been blessed with a great sense of humor, and had kept busy and hopeful meeting all these challenges. She said, "I passed poverty with an "A" and have a government loan to fix up my house like new. Life is beautiful, and I am enclosing a picture of me on my first parachute dive - on my 80th birthday!" What a lift that woman gave to everyone who received one of her greeting cards.

• FEAR OF NOT BEING OF VALUE OR WORTH. My children grew up with the philosophy that "you are not just here to fill up space, but to make a difference" and each one has, in his or her own way. I have always loved this statement from scripture, and it comforts and reassures when there is a tendency to feel nonproductive and self-centered. "And what does the Lord require of you . . . but to do justly, to love mercy, and to walk humbly with your God." Everyone of us can measure up to that simple standard. In his excellent new book, 'Prayer, My Soul's Adventure With God,' Dr. Robert Schuller suggests this catchy little prayer with which to start one's day. I have been using it daily, with some rather astounding results. "Good Morning, God . . . What are you up to today? Can I be a part of it? Thank you, Amen." All fear of irrelevance disappears when we accept that kind of assignment!

Many of us grew up in a time when every teacher, every preacher, assured us that the greatest days were yet to be, and we were thrilled by it. Now we seem to have come upon strange, often sad times when faith and belief in the future seem to have been lost by multitudes of people. Of course, we can look back and see many of the ways we have helped to contribute to the disillusionment, but the backward look is never the answer, except to see what didn't work and not to repeat it. These days we need to surround ourselves with people who believe in us and in the future, and we need to be there for those who can benefit from our optimism and faith in a better world. Getting rid of our fears and anxieties is one step in being a force for good. My congregation used to grow weary of my saying, maybe too often, "You can never give out of an empty hand." But I always recognized the need to feel full and supplied and eager to share before I could ever bring them messages of hope and promise. Consider this New Year's greeting as our gift to you, recognizing your worth and value as a spiritual being, reminding you to look for the good in all people and all conditions, regardless of appearance. Maybe that is why we are so geared to saying, "Happy New Year," with such enthusiasm - we are serving as reminders to others of the good that life holds for them.

When the famous Marx Brothers were in the early stages of their career, the family home was heavily mortgaged to the Greenbaum Bank. Often the payments were hard to come by. So, when the brothers were performing on stage, their mother would stand in the wings, and whenever her zany sons would stray from the script, she would quickly snap them back to reality with a loud stage whisper, GREENBAUM, REMEMBER GREENBAUM.

My friends, remember who you are and why you are here. Have a wonderful 1996, with all the blessings a giving universe can bestow upon you!.

[January 1996]

AND IT CAME TO PASS. . .

A story from the ancient past tells of a monarch who called his wise men to him one day, and asked them for a motto, or some magic words, which would help him face the challenges in his life. The motto must be short enough to engrave on the inside of a ring. The wise men deliberated for days, knowing that their lives were at stake should they fail to come up with a suitable motto. Finally, they submitted their choice, and it pleased the monarch, who rewarded them lavishly. These simple words can be a fitting and useful motto for our complicated, challenging lives today. They were: THIS TOO SHALL PASS.

I have no answer for the question I hear, over and over. "Why do there seem to be so many more problems, tragedies, accidents, and unexpected happenings at this time of year?" Perhaps you have wondered about this too. I have found real comfort and courage in the four words on the monarch's ring, and I remember them often when faced with some unexpected, often unpleasant, emergency. Somehow the words bring a sense of perspective and proportion, and allow me to move through the experience with more poise and equanimity.

A little boy was afraid of tunnels. When he rode in the car with his parents, or while he was on a train trip to visit grandparents, he always hid his face in his mother's lap, or squeezed his eyes tightly shut. One day he discovered that tunnels were not as scary as he had thought. One day he actually told his mother that now he liked tunnels because, in his words, "they have light at both ends."

I have always been fascinated in observing how people handle the same experience . . . one may accept the tunnel experience as if it were a permanent, static condition, while the other person, faced with identical circumstances, moves through the situation with balance and comfort knowing that there is always light at the end of his or her particular tunnel, that no tunnel lasts forever. Such a person, like the famous battery-bunny, keeps on going and going, and in the keeping on finds his greatest growth and improvement.

We all know people who have allowed physical handicaps to make weaklings and cowards of them. Great disappointments and misfortunes have caused many to give up, to take permanent residency in the valley of the shadow of self-pity and bitterness. Thank God, there are others like Beethoven and Helen Keller who have passed through the dark tunnel of adversity and have reached new heights of achievement and victory.

No one that I know is immune from serious challenges at some time or other. My first suggestion for handling those "lemons" is to refuse to give in to panic, keep as cool and collected as possible. I often use this affirmation in such instances, "I recognize the appearance of this problem, but not its permanence. It came in order to teach me some valuable lesson and then to pass on through my life experience. I accept the gift it brings and move on." Can you believe that every cloud has a silver lining? This is not just a pretty cliché, a Pollyanna-type sedative. It is the truth, and accepting it as a truth, a principle, will make all the difference in the way you handle your problems.

Try to remember what you were troubled about a year ago, or even six months ago. Where is the problem now? Where are all the people who seemed to stand in the way of your good? Francois Villon once said, "Where are the snows of yesteryear?" Now, obliviously the snows and rains of yesteryear have become part of oceans and rivers, plants and trees. All of these have become part of new life and new forms. They have all served some useful purpose.

A man sentenced to prison for five years was bitter and vindictive and filled with self-pity. He knew he had committed a crime for which he had to pay, but he could not relate to the kind of people with whom he had to live in prison. The general atmosphere of the place depressed him and he resented every one. Some of his fellow prisoners tried to be friendly, but he ignored them. One day he met a trustee who was honest and frank with him. "Look here," his new friend said. "If you start to do something worthwhile these five years will pass before you know it. Why not spend your time getting ready for the day you'll get out. Your time here can be as useful as a college education. Try meeting people in a more friendly manner. Make an effort to get along." The words made sense to the down - hearted fellow, and he began to change. He enrolled in a class in radio repairing. He got along so well, and became so engrossed in his studies that he could hardly wait for each day's class. At the end of 4 years, he was paroled for good behavior. Today that man is a highly respected, well paid specialist in the electronics profession. His time as a prisoner came to pass, not to stay, and four little words contributed much to his success in life.

I once saw a man wearing a button from the New York World's Fair. The button said, "I WAS THERE." It was rather sad to see that that old button was his one claim to importance in life, but lots of us wear similar medals in the form of press clippings, trophies, group pictures on the wall. There is nothing wrong with healthy nostalgia. It is good to look back on, and appreciate the blessings that have come our way, but as some one once remarked to a friend, "We may become so fond of riding the observation car that we see only where we have been, never where we are going."

This new year, with its ups and downs, its unexpected events and surprises, can be infinitely more rewarding and pleasant if we will remember that a tunnel has light at both ends, and that whatever the experience, it came to pass, not to stay.

God bless.

[February 1996]

BE SOMEONE'S SILVER LINING

"That to which you give your attention tends to increase and multiply. . ."

If you listen to conversations around you these days, you might conclude that the times in which we are living are the most troublesome and difficult in history, that the pressures and challenges we face are new and unique to modern life. Read these quotes and their surprising sources:

"I'm in difficulty, both summer and winter, about my salary."
> --An Egyptian worker in 256 B.C.

"The first of June, and nothing done by the Senate."
> --Cicero 38 B.C.

"Athletics have become professionalized."
> --Socrates 402 BC

So, what is new? Human beings are still facing the same problems faced by our ancestors. The names or descriptions may have changed, but the essence is the same. None of us, at any stage in history, is protected from the downs of life, large or small. You may be president of your company with a big income, all the advantages that go with prestige and authority. The stockholders hold a meeting, decide to merge with a larger company and, since yours is the smaller company, you are out of a job. You're a teacher with tenure. The enrollment drops off and you are no longer needed. . . You are married and go off to work one morning, unaware of impending trouble, and return home that night to find your relationship in crisis. You've taken your good health for granted when suddenly a tumor appears and your life is threatened.

There are two ways to handle these unexpected happenings. One is to ask, "Why me?" There is confusion and fear, and the reminder that bad things do happen to good people. A minister friend once shared this humorous story with a group of ministers: "I know why some people like church. It is the one place where bad things can't happen to them for one hour in the whole week. The sink won't run over, the phone won't ring, the school principal can't call to say he's got your son in his office for some misbehavior. No downers can happen during the service. The only price you pay for that hour of bliss is the possibility of being bored to death by the sermon."

The second way to handle life's ups and downs is to be aware that life proceeds like a sine wave, the line on a graph that looks like a continuous undulating wave. The good news is that you and I have the power to draw the zero point through our sine wave. Everything below is bad and everything above is good. Depending on where you place your zero point, you can have lots of uppers or endless downers. Example: One person will say, "When I went downtown today, I just knew I'd find a good parking space and I did, only two blocks away, and right in front of a shop where I had another purchase to make. What a miracle. The other person will say "I prayed for a parking place and three other people got closer to the front door than I did . . . what a bummer!" Now, what constitutes a miracle for you? How convenient must your parking place be before you rate it as an upper or a downer? Here are some suggestions for adjusting your zero line:

• REMEMBER PAST SUCCESSES. Everyone has some. You haven't always been discouraged or in trouble or sick.

• REMEMBER THAT "THIS TOO SHALL PASS." Nothing lasts forever except the eternal verities of God's love and guidance and support. A sense of perspective is essential in handling troubles. When you and I move through the difficult times with courage and faith in the ultimate good, all humanity is blessed. Our being miserable is no blessing to anyone else. On the contrary, the more successful and fulfilled we are the more we reflect our divine nature, and the more good we draw to us.

• GET INVOLVED IN SOMETHING CONSTRUCTIVE. Energy follows thought, so that to which you give your attention tends to increase and multiply. Put your time and thought and energy into something positive and worthwhile.

• DO SOMETHING FOR SOMEONE ELSE. This need to get out of one's own misery has been the motivation for many wonderful movements and organizations--Mothers Against Drunk Driving, groups dedicated to finding lost children, agencies for meeting the needs of victims of various diseases. Just consider the good that has come out of seeming tragedies. We have recently observed the 10th anniversary of the Challenger tragedy, in which seven very special people lost their lives in space. I heartily recommend a new book, Silver Linings, by June Scobie Rogers, the widow of Dick Scobie, the shuttle's commander. This remarkable woman, aided by the families of the other victims of the catastrophe, has established over thirty centers throughout the country, where children and young people can use their fertile minds to find answers to deep questions about space travel, communication, team work... What a memorial to those seven astronauts!

In less dramatic ways, but with as much significance and importance on a human level, you and I can move through our grief and fear and concern about issues in our lives. We can reach out and touch someone with love and understanding, and find, to our amazement, that our own pain is lessened, and that the energy we would have given to self-pity and hopelessness is used as a silver lining to someone else's cloud.

[March 1996]

FEARLESS FAITH FACES FACTS

What is faith? Where did it come from? Faith is just a word to many, but actually it is an action word, a verb. The truth is that you were born with it. You took your first step in faith. A hand was held out to you and you moved to take that hand in yours. You marry with faith in the one you have chosen. You drive or ride the bus to work, expecting to arrive. You eat food prepared by hands you will never see. You make plans for a vacation fully expecting to be able to carry out those plans. Faith is a sunflower facing the sun. It is the ear at the telephone. We never perfect our faith by talking or reading, or waiting or wishing, but only by applying it to every phase of living. Faith opens the way for power to flow in. There is a vast difference between hope and faith. Hope says that something might happen. Faith says that something WILL happen. What is faith? It is the confident assurance that something we want is going to happen, even though we see no sign of it up ahead.

Faith is like a muscle. Without use it atrophies and becomes useless or non-existent. The Bible tells us that faith without works is dead. The Bible is full of exciting examples of faith and the mountains of problems and difficulties it dissolved in the lives of real people. In the story of Abraham God told Abraham to leave the comfortable life he knew, and to go to a place to which God would lead him. Abraham, a pillar of faith, packed up his large family, all his immense possessions, his servants, his herds of animals - a monumental job in the days before U-Haul trucking services, and went, not knowing where he was going. Now, that is faith in action. The sick woman who touched the hem of Jesus' garment in the crowd was instantly healed, when Jesus said, "Your faith has made you whole." He didn't say that his mighty power had healed her, but that her simple but complete faith had provided the conditions for a complete healing.

The statement that faith without works is dead

reminds me of the story of the little girl learning to ride a bicycle, with some difficulty and several falls. Finally she said, "God, if you'll just give me a push, I'll do the pedaling." That is the secret to the miracle working power of faith. The little girl didn't expect God to do it all, just to start her out right, then she would do her part by "acting as if" she couldn't fail.

The famous Babe Ruth story is a perfect example of faith in action. You know the particulars. . . The Babe had hit one home run in the game, now with two strikes against him, he raised his hand and pointed over the fence. With a crack of the bat, the ball sailed in a perfect arc to the exact spot to which he had pointed. Pandemonium broke out. Later someone asked him, "But suppose you had missed the final strike?" A look of amazement came over the Babe's face and he answered, "Why, I never thought of such a thing!"

This little story illustrates a profound law; namely, that when you take into your mind the thought of impossibility, you tend to create the conditions of impossibility. Prior to the formation of such a negative thought, your entire being, body, mind, and spirit, works as a unity in perfect harmony. The powerful forces of the universe are flowing through your personality. But when you change the cast and slant of your mind so that you hold the idea of the impossible, you tend to block off in yourself the continued flow of coordinated power. You become rigid and tightened up and the easy flow of power is diverted or completely destroyed. In every endeavor of your life, your skills and abilities will be depleted when doubt takes the upper hand in your thinking and feeling. I liken this to standing on the hose when you are trying to water your yard. The water is coming freely and fully out of the spigot, backed up by your connection to the town water supply, which in turn is connected to a larger reservoir which can take care of all the needs of the community. How is the flow through your hose impeded? By you, standing on the hose, in just the same way, we hold up the good we desire in our lives through lack of belief, a scarcity of faith, by giving in to doubt and apprehension. Faith can move mountains, and that is not just a pretty platitude -- it does, in incredible ways.

A man was diagnosed with cancer of the throat. He was illiterate, ignorant of medical terms and procedures. One day a nurse put a thermometer in his mouth. He believed it was some kind of x-ray that would cure him. The wise doctor, observing the man's reaction, decided to leave the thermometer in longer than usual, then he told the man to get dressed and come back a few days later. After three treatments with the thermometer, the man was completely healed, never to suffer from the disease again. The thermometer didn't do it - faith did.

During a heavy storm at sea the captain said to the frightened passengers, "We must have faith." A terrified woman rushed up to the captain and cried out, "Captain, are we really in danger?" to which the calm captain replied, "Don't worry, madam. After all we are in the hands of God." "O dear," she sighed. "Is it as bad as that?"

In the delightful little book, God's Little Chicken Soup for the Spirit, the authors share this bit of wisdom-- remember that the faith that moves mountains, always carries a pick, which is another way of saying that faith without work is dead. Remember, that the more you use the faculty of faith, the stronger and more valuable and useful it becomes.

God bless you.

[August 1996]

ADVENTURES IN INDIA

Without leaving the planet, I have just spent three weeks in another world, a world without phones, newspapers, radio, or TV, or any of the other distractions that claim so much of our energy and attention. That other world was the tiny village of Puttaparti, in southern India, where I went with three dear friends to find out for myself the truth or fallacy of a little brown man, whose message of love and service and transformation of consciousness is sweeping the world. Through some marvelous quirk of fate last winter, I received a personal invitation from Sathya Sai Baba to visit his ashram. So, on the 31st of July I found myself transported, via Hong Kong, Bombay, and Bangalore to a place that defies description.

Twice a day for 18 days I sat with thousands of women, men and children from all over the world in a huge, covered, open-air arena, as the small orange clad figure moved through the quiet, orderly crowd, stopping here and there for a word of blessing, a helpful message to some eager devotee. There were groups from all over the world, and the words Sai Baba spoke were always in the appropriate language. Each day a very few individuals were chosen to join the avatar in his private interview room, where he showed an uncanny knowledge of the life and experience of each person, and where he offered loving counsel and showered upon all his unconditional love, now and then producing from his empty hand a precious gemstone ring, or locket or necklace which he gave to the grateful recipient.

I spent much time with people who live at the ashram and witnessed the wonders of this incredible being on a daily basis. All the claims of his divinity, the obvious signs and wonders that surround him constantly were confirmed and verified by the many new friends who shared their amazing experiences with me. It was my great privilege to have two audiences with him and to experience, as never before, the power of pure love in expression.

His words to me were reassuring and comforting and the time spent in his presence was more than worth the inconveniences and discomforts of life in the ashram, and the temporary physical ailments which seem to be part of life in that part of the world.

This is not an attempt to convince anyone of anything. It is simply the description of an experience which was so deep and profound and personally transforming that I want to share it. I came home tired from the rigors of the trip, and more peaceful and in love with life than ever before. I am also motivated to spend the rest of my life living more fully the teachings of Sai Baba, which are also the teachings of Jesus Christ, and of all great spiritual leaders who have ever lived.

Baba says, "My life is my message . . . love all, serve all." Kahlil Gibran said, "Let your daily life by your religion." Jesus said, "If you know these things, blessed are you if you do them."

If you are trying to make sense of this confusing world, if you search for answers in a world which offers very few satisfying ones in these difficult times, perhaps you would like to join me in a simple project - that of being aware of your own divinity and living from the knowing. Jesus said, "Ye are all gods, all sons of the most high." Sai Baba says, "You are your own guru-divinity living within you." Along with desire to simplify my life, I have also rededicated my life to love, to consciously experiencing God's love in every waking moment, to look for evidences of that love in everyone and everything that comes into my life.

One of the very tangible and very important aspects of Sai Baba's work is his service to the world. I witnessed, first hand, the amazing transformation taking place in the lives of young people through his Human Values Education programs, now included in the curriculum of every public school in India, and incidentally a program which is desperately needed in this country. It is based on the principles of truth, self-reliance, responsibility, honesty, integrity, love, peace and non-violence, among other powerful concepts. I saw hundreds of young people who are the recipients of this kind of training. Their scholastic records are the highest in the nation and the universal, non-denominational spiritual principles they are learning will enable them to take responsible positions in adult life.

In every major city of India are free food centers, medical clinics, job placement centers, all staffed by volunteer Sai Baba devotees. I talked with a young man from Bosnia who told me, first hand, of the relief work being done in his ravaged country by Sai volunteers. No one, of the vast Sai organization, is paid a penny - all serve for the love of serving and, of course, reap the inevitable rewards of such service in tangible and intangible ways.

I came back to Ashland this week, physically tired, but mentally and emotionally charged with new purpose and new determination to make the remaining years of my life the best of my whole life.

[September 1996]

THE URGENCY OF CHANGE

Have you heard the story about the Board meeting that Satan is supposed to have called in Hell? He put this question to his senior advisors: "We need to develop a new strategy for causing havoc on earth. Any suggestions for a new way to reach human beings for our side?" One advisor offered this method: "Tell the people there is no heaven." Another said: "Tell them there is no hell." But the prize-winning solution was this: "Tell them there is no hurry."

I suggest that there are three distinct areas that need our attention. They are personal relationships, our habits and dependencies, and our role in the cosmic order of things.

In the first category, who of us could not benefit from some improvement? There is an urgency in expressing our affection for the people in our lives. Children grow up so quickly, loved ones pass on or move to another part of the country. Someone once remarked that if there were suddenly a radio announcement that the world would end in an hour, every phone booth would be jammed with people wanting to call someone to say "I love you." Can you think of at least one person for whom you care deeply, who doesn't really know how you feel about him/her?

I have a friend who was given just six months to live, and she spent those precious months getting in touch with people, those dear to her and those with whom she had had difficulties. She wrote a long, loving, honest letter to her sister who had treated her badly; she wrote to a politician, apologizing for the nasty, harsh letters she had sent him. She wrote letters to everyone on her Christmas card list, saying good-bye and expressing her appreciation for their friendship. Finally, all the loose ends were neatly taken care of, and she told me that she felt so relieved and confident that she was going into her new life with no strings attached. Six months passed, and with them her disease. That six-month verdict was 20 years ago.

The second area which calls for urgency is that of our lifestyle. When life seems not to be in harmony, when we are troubled time after time with the same problems, life is telling us that it is time for a change. The change might be minor or it might be drastic. How many of us wake up to find that it is too late to save a damaged friendship, recover a lost opportunity, save an ailing marriage? Change can be scary, but as a wise one once said, "The greatest risk is not to risk."

Years ago, I made notes on a book, the title of which I do not remember, so my apologies to the author, who wrote: "To doubt is spiritually fatal. When you doubt the Creator's plan for your life, the soul is stymied, the life is wasted. Spirit is free, active, unlimited. Doubt keeps the Spirit's full expression locked into a tiny, dark cell, without breath to live, all possibilities doomed. For it is only in your willingness to trust the unseen that you grow!"

In the Peanuts cartoon, Linus, the team statistician, brings Charlie Brown, the manager, his report, which reads; "In 12 games we almost scored a run, and in 9 games the other team almost didn't score before the 1st out. In right field, Lucy almost caught 23 balls, and once almost made the right play." With a sigh, Linus concludes, "We led the league in almosts, Charlie Brown."

In a book entitled Staying O.K., the author lists 9 obstacles in making the best use of our time. They are: 1. simply 'things,' 2. not saying no, 3. unmade decisions, 4. television, 5. lack of planning, 6. being surrounded with clutter, 7. ignoring maintenance, 8. idle waiting, 9. worrying about the future.

All of these obstacles have a familiar ring, but perhaps the greatest deterrent is that sometimes our lives have no center, no driving purpose, no grand aspiration.

The third reason for the urgency of change is the world's need. Continuing my notes from the book I mentioned earlier:
"Since the earth itself is a unique being who is growing and learning, as do all things in the universe, you affect

her by the way you treat her, by the type of care you give. You have filled her emotions with such violence and terror, it is no wonder you fear volcanoes and earthquakes and the trembling of that mighty one on which you ride. She has the power to shrug, itch, scratch, and eliminate those non-caring thoughts and actions given to her by individuals and combined humanity. This is your time to give to the earth that which will nourish and support.

Love yourself as the beautiful light that was created for the Creator's pleasure long ago. Love all others of the mineral, plant, animal, and human family. There are many who guide and protect you when you practice love."

Examine your day. Are you caught up in the stressful push for a life that lacks a spiritual expression of love? If so, make the necessary changes now. Surrender your doubts and judgments and let the higher powers assist humanity in its planned ascension. The time is now. You are not alone.

<u>Other Books by Margaret Stevens</u>

Prosperity is God's Idea

You Cannot Die

<u>Books for children</u>

Stepping Stones for Little Feet
Stepping Stones for Boys and Girls
Stepping Stones #2

DeVross & Co., Publishers
Marina del Rey, California
©1987

Cancer: A Tool for Transformation
One woman's journey from Fear to Fulfillment.

The Margaret Stevens Institute
P.O. Box 3366
Ashland, Oregon 97520

541-482-6115